174

The Demon

A Thriller

Martin Downing

Samuel French—London
New York-Toronto-Hollywood

THE DEMON

First performed at The Urdang Academy of Ballet and Performing Arts, Covent Garden, with the following cast of characters:

Matt	Philip Willingham
Vicky	Sarah Kirton
Emma	Michele Sidwell
Guy	Martin Downing
Dave	Sam McAvoy
Corinne	Ysabelle Carter-Griffiths
Lucia	Elizabeth Blindell

The action takes place in Matt and Vicky's flat on the sixth floor of an apartment block on a dark and stormy night

Time—the present

CHARACTERS

Matt	A businessman
Vicky	Matt's wife
Emma	Vicky's friend
Guy	Matt's colleague
Dave	Matt's colleague
Corinne	Dave's girlfriend
Lucia	Matt and Vicky's neighbour

Also by Martin Downing published by Samuel French Ltd

The House of Dracula
The House of Frankenstein!
Out For The Count

To my brother Michael — with love

Matt and Vicky's living-room on the sixth floor of an apartment block

It is a good-sized room, simply but comfortably furnished. UC *are a pair of floor-length curtains obviously concealing a window casement. On either side shelf units support hi-fi equipment, objets d' art and a collection of drinks and glasses.* UR *a doorway leads to the entrance hall.* UL *and* DL *lockable doors give access to the kitchen and bedrooms*

A bookcase stands against the wall L *on top of which is an attractive modern clock. Over* R *next to the doorway is a wall phone. A two-seater sofa stands to the right of* C. *Behind the sofa is a table supporting photographs and a carved wooden box which contains a crucifix. There are also two armchairs and side tables* L *and* DR *respectively. The walls are decorated with a number of framed prints. A rug lies in front of the sofa and there is a pendant light above* L

When the CURTAIN *rises, the pendant light is on and heavy rain can be heard lashing against the unseen windows. This doesn't need to be continuous, but can be added into the later action if desired*

Vicky, a quiet, unassuming woman in her mid-thirties is standing UC *listening to Guy, who is off* R. *Her manner is strangely tense*

Guy (*off*) Hey, Vicky — this coat's drenched! Have you got anything to catch the drips?

Vicky Use that bath towel. The one by the umbrellas.

Guy (*off*) Oh yeah. Don't want to start the night by ruining your carpet.

He enters from R *, drying his hands on his trousers , a good looking, easy-going man, also in his thirties*

Vicky (*staring at him*)You're early.

Guy (*glancing at his watch*) So I am. (*He frowns slightly*)Sorry — I didn't catch you in the middle of something, did I?

Vicky (*hesitantly*)No. It's just that Matt's out at the off-licence and—

Guy (*smiling faintly*)You don't like being alone with his unmarried mates.

Vicky (*quickly*)Don't be silly. I'll have trouble giving you a drink, that's all.

Guy You've run out of gin?

Vicky (*shaking her head*)Tonic water.

Guy (*grinning*)No problem there. I'll drink it neat, for now.

Vicky moves to pour him his drink as he stands listening to the rain outside

Guy (*grimacing*)Great weather for ducks, eh?

Vicky (*dryly*)Terrific.

Guy (*slowly*) Or " slimy things that crawl with legs upon the slimy sea..."

Vicky (*turning to him, glass in hand*)Sorry?

Guy (*rousing himself*)It's from " The Rime of the Ancient Mariner."

Vicky (*realizing*) Oh yes.

Guy You know it?

Vicky I did it years ago — at school.

Guy (*wryly*)Didn't we all? (*Musing*) Pretty horrific, too — all that stuff about the living dead. It's a wonder we didn't have nightmares.

Vicky Some of us probably did. D'you want ice?

Guy I wouldn't mind.

Vicky Well, I'm afraid it's still in the fridge. (*She offers him his glass, awkwardly*)Would you like to —?

Guy (*taking it, affably*)Sure. (*He starts moving towards the door up* L)Shall I fill up a bucket?

Vicky Good idea. You know where they are?

He nods and opens the door

Thanks, Guy.

Guy (*turning with a smile*)Don't mention it. (*As he goes*)" The ice was here, the ice was there, the ice was all around: It cracked and growled, and roared and howled..."

Vicky listens to him, her face strangely serious and then turns as the buzzer sounds off R

Vicky (*moving* R *and calling off*) Coming!

She disappears through the doorway and we hear the sound of the door being opened

Vicky (*off*)Hello, Em.

Emma (*off; fervently*) God, what a night! We should be building an ark!

Vicky (*off*) I know. But where can you do a crash-course in carpentry?

Emma (*off*) The local Tech.? Be careful with that. It's soaked.

Vicky (*off*) So I see.

At this point Emma enters shaking the rain out of her hair; a lively, cheerful young woman, slightly younger than Vicky

Emma I tell you, if it hadn't been one of your do's, I'd have stayed in and read my book.

Vicky enters wiping her hands

Vicky I wouldn't have blamed you. What's the latest?

Emma *The Madman and the Nun.*

Vicky Sounds lively.

Emma I doubt it. The cover's bound to be the best part. (*She pauses*) Who else is here?

Vicky Just Guy — being poetic.

Emma smiles

But Dave and Corinne can't be far behind. You know what he's like for free booze.

Emma (*grimacing*) It's what he's like *after* it. The last time we were here I spent all night with my back to the wall!

Vicky (*mischievously*) Isn't that how he likes it?

Emma Dave? I'd say *no* holds are barred.

Vicky Every Which Way That's Loose!

They both laugh. Then Emma moves to sit on the sofa

Emma Seriously, though, he can be a real animal. Why does Matt keep inviting him?

Vicky hesitates

I know they work together, but—
Vicky It's not just that. They're old friends — like us. And Matt — well, he says Dave wasn't always like that.
Emma (*sceptically*) You're kidding!
Vicky (*quickly*) It's this last year that's changed him.
Emma Well, I don't see why, when he's got Corinne to keep him happy.(*Pointedly*)Or doesn't she?
Vicky (*wryly*) *He* says she does — so it must be the same old story.
Emma (*emphatically*) He likes a bit more on the side! (*She shakes her head*)How on earth does she put up with it?
Vicky (*moving to the drinks*)By gritting her teeth and thinking of his salary?

Emma raises an eyebrow

I doubt if she'd do more. She's not what you'd call a fighter.
Emma No.
Vicky And even if she were, Dave is and always will be the boss.

She moves to hand Emma a glass of sweet Martini

Your usual, madam.
Emma Thanks. (*She glances up*)Well, *I* think she's a fool. If a man of mine played around the way he does, I'd sever much more than our relationship!

She mimes snipping with a pair of scissors

Vicky (*smiling*)You wouldn't!
Emma Want to bet ? If Dave tries any of his lechy little tricks

tonight —

The door buzzer sounds again and Vicky moves UR

Vicky Ssh! That might be him now.
Emma Good! Where d'you keep your scissors?
Vicky (*grinning*) Emma.

She disappears off R

Emma sips her drink and we hear the door open

Vicky (*off*) Oh, it's you. What took you so long?
Matt (*off; gruffly*) I got held back. Can you take this for me?
Vicky (*off*) Yes, but I needed you here. I can't manage every-
thing, you know.
Matt (*off*) Vicky...

*Vicky enters holding a carrier bag which contains mixers for
drinks. Matt follows her, a rugged, well-built man, aged about
forty. He is not just wet, but also very tense*

Vicky (*turning to him as she puts the bottles with the rest*) Where
did you stop off? The Three Crowns?
Matt I wish to God I *had*.
Vicky (*sensing his mood*) Why?
Matt (*gravely*) There's been another murder.

Vicky and Emma react

Down in the subway. That's what kept me. (*He grimaces*) Talk
about chaos! The police were all over the place. (*He suddenly
notices Emma*) Sorry, Em. I didn't know you were —

Emma (*faintly*)It's OK.

Matt (*turning back to Vicky*)They thought I might have been a witness.

Vicky (*warily*)And were you?

Matt (*shaking his head*)But it was a close thing. The girl had only just been killed.

Emma (*curiously*)You saw her?

Matt (*hesitating*)No. She was covered up, at the bottom of the steps.

Emma (*pointedly*)Then how d'you know it was a girl?

Matt and Vicky exchange glances, then he turns back to Emma

Matt (*with an effort*)I don't. I just assumed that. Because of the others — and the *way* she'd been killed.

Emma (*faintly*)The way —?

Matt (*gravely*)There was blood everywhere.

He holds out his right hand which is clearly blood-stained and the others recoil

I bumped into one of the guys who'd touched her.

Emma (*horrified*)Oh Matt!

Matt He was a right mess. (*He stares at his hand*) Jesus.

Vicky (*moving to him; gently*)You'd better wash that off — (*She glances at Emma*)—or our *other* guests might get suspicious.

Emma (*frowning*)Vicky...

Vicky (*lightly*)Only joking.

Matt moves down L

(*To Matt*) Shall I fix you a drink?

Matt Yes. And make it a large one — eh, love?

She nods

   Guy enters with his glass and ice-bucket

Guy (*seeing Matt; brightly*)Hi, partner! How's it hanging?
Matt (*gruffly*)Bloody badly!

   He exits down L *leaving Guy staring after him, puzzled*

Guy What's up with him?
Vicky (*awkwardly; taking the ice-bucket from him*)He's ... had
   a bad shock.
Guy (*grinning*)The cops spotted his tax-disc?
Emma (*exchanging glances with Vicky*)He's just seen a dead
   body.
Guy (*wide-eyed*)Whose?
Vicky (*putting the ice-bucket* UL)Another murder victim.
Guy (*slowly*)That serial killer again?
Vicky (*nodding*)It looks like it.
Guy Christ! That's the fourth, isn't it? When's the bastard going
   to stop?
Vicky (*staring at him*)Tonight, maybe.
Guy (*puzzled*)What?

The door buzzer sounds again

   Vicky goes to answer it

 *Guy stares after her, then moves to top up his drink with tonic
water. Emma turns towards the doorway* UR *as Vicky opens the
door and Corinne and Dave's voices are heard off*

Corinne (*off*)But you shouldn't have been so *rude*.

Dave (*off; slightly slurred*)I don't like crack-pots! 'Specially when they sneak up on you. Anyway, I came here for a party, not a damn lecture! Hello, Vicky.

Vicky (*off; disconcerted*)Hi.

Corinne (*off; interrupting*)Even so.

Vicky (*off*)What's been going on?

Dave(*off*)Corinne'll tell you. I'm going to get me a drink.

Dave enters UR. *He is a reasonably handsome man who is now going to seed. He grins at Guy and Emma as he heads for the whisky bottle*

Dave Hello, you lot.

Guy and Emma reply in kind, exchanging knowing glances

Vicky and Corinne enter. Corinne is a dark, slightly exotic girl, clearly a lot younger them Dave. She carries an evening bag

Vicky (*prompting her*)Well?

Corinne (*sighing and moving to sit to Emma's right on the sofa*) Dave and I ran into some woman down in the foyer.

Dave (*turning*)Wrong! She ran into us.

Corinne Whatever. And she — (*She hesitates*)Well, she gave Dave a warning.

Guy (*moving to sit in the armchair* DR)To give up the booze, right?

Dave (*taking a mouthful of whisky, shaking his head*)Uh-uh.

Vicky What then?

Dave (*before Corinne can speak*) She said the devil will get me, if I'm not careful.

Guy (*grinning*) Same thing, I'd say.
Corinne(*sharply*)Not quite.

*Matt enters DL and listens to them warily. Vicky glances at him
cautiously*

Emma (*curious*) What did she look like?
Dave (*emphatically*)Weird, Emma. Weird!

He knocks back his drink, then pours himself another

Emma (*dryly*)That's a great help.
Corinne (*quickly*)She was wearing a long dress — a bit like a
    caftan, with lots of chains and amulets round her neck.
Dave In other words, weird.
Corinne (*ignoring him*)And she spoke with a foreign accent.
Dave (*smugly*)Which is why I told her to push off and go and tell
    horror stories in her own country!

*He laughs and eyes Emma appreciatively as he moves to sit in the
armchair L. Vicky goes to pour drinks for herself, Matt and
Corinne*

Emma (*returning Dave's gaze impassively*)And where's that
    exactly?
Dave (*shrugging*)Romania, or some other God forsaken state.
Vicky (*handing Matt a whisky*)Actually, she was born here like
    the rest of us. It's her parents who're foreign.
Corinne You know her then?
Vicky (*handing her a drink*)Yes. Her name's Lucia Ciprian and
    she's one of our neighbours.
Dave (*dryly*)Lucky you!
Matt (*staring at him*)What did she say when you told her to get

lost?

Dave That it's only fools who scoff at the truth, but since most men are, it's no wonder evil things escape discovery. And get this — she's sure my days are numbered.

Emma (*sharply*)What d'you mean?

Dave (*emphatically*)I'm going to come to a horrible end — at the hands of some unearthly spirit!

Corinne Have you ever heard anything so ridiculous?

Dave *She'll* be pushing up daisies before any devil gets me — you can be sure of that! (*He knocks back his drink, then holds up the glass*)Same again, barman!

Matt takes his glass and goes to the whisky bottle, exchanging glances with Vicky as she moves DR *with her own drink*

Vicky (*slowly*)There's something you should know, Dave. Dr Ciprian is an expert on the occult.

Corinne *Doctor* Ciprian?

Vicky (*nodding*)She got a Ph.D in folklore — but then went on to study black magic.

Emma What on earth for?

Matt (*returning with Dave's glass*)Because she felt sure that a great many supernatural phenomena aren't unrelated occurrences. They're manifestations of a single demonic force. And when her research confirmed this, she decided to set about protecting the rest of us — sceptical though we are.

Dave Sceptical's right. The woman's cracked!

Vicky (*evenly*)She isn't, Dave.

Corinne Oh, come on! She was babbling on about planetary alignment, full moons and God knows what!

Dave (*grinning*)And if I don't say my prayers like a good boy —

Guy (*wryly*)Count Dracula will drop by to sink his fangs in your neck. (*Musing*)The thing is — can drunk vampires *fly*?

Corinne (*sternly*)*Guy.*

He laughs lightly, then turns to Vicky, whose face is serious

Guy What's up? You're not telling me you believe all this crap?
Vicky (*hesitantly*)No — I don't think so.
Guy Then why are you frowning?
Vicky (*slowly*)Lucia claims she's psychic. When any of the
  elementals come near her, she can usually sense them.
Emma Forgive my ignorance, but what's an elemental?
Matt An evil spirit which attaches itself to a human host.
Dave You're kidding!

Matt shakes his head gravely

  Does the host *know* when one of these things comes to stay?
Matt (*hesitating*)I'm not sure. But what attracts it is the person's
  capacity for cruelty. That's what it feeds off, and in return it
  drives the person to be even more cruel.
Emma (*dryly*)Charming.
Corinne (*sharply*)But why is she so worried about Dave?
Vicky (*slowly*) I think she's worried about all of us.
Guy How come?
Vicky Because tonight, as she told you, several of the supposedly
  malign planets have come into conjunction, and there's also a
  full moon, which gives elementals enormous strength.
Guy (*grinning*)Together with fur, fangs and a long snout!

Dave laughs but the others remain straight-faced

Matt (*pointedly*)And she thinks there's one with us — right now.

There is a frozen silence

Corinne(*wide-eyed*)But how could she possibly —
Matt (*quickly but firmly*)Vicky and I have thrown three parties
this year and you've all come to them. Right?

They nod their agreement

Well the next day, or slightly later, Dr Ciprian would pop up to
see us — about the Residents' Committee or to borrow something.

He exchanges glances with Vicky

But it wasn't till her third visit that we learned the *real* reason
for her calling. (*He pauses*)She wanted to confirm that an evil
spirit had been present in our flat.
Emma (*faintly*)And did she?
Matt Oh yes. But the traces were always very faint. She could
never identify who'd left them.

*He hesitates, glancing at everyone in turn, stopping when he
reaches Guy*

So we decided to arrange this meeting tonight.
Corinne (*rising; fearfully*)You mean she thinks one of us is
possessed?
Matt (*evenly*) I'm afraid so. (*He stares at them uncertainly*) She
also thinks they're the serial killer the police are after.

There is an incredulous pause

Guy (*unbelieving*)What?!

Dave guffaws with laughter

Dave If you believe that, boy, you need a holiday!(*He taps his temple*)And that Doctor what's-her-name of yours should be locked up. Pronto!

3 SECONDS BLACK OUT

He laughs again and Matt knocks back his drink with a mixture of embarrassment and annoyance. The others, though, are silent and serious as Matt turns away from them to refill his glass—and as he does so the lights flicker and then go out. In the darkness Vicky moves to the door UL,*Corinne moves* DR,*and Guy moves to the doorway* UR

Matt }   (*together*)   { What the blazes — ?
Emma }   { Oh!

Corinne (*nervously*)Is someone playing games?

Vicky No — it's just a power-cut, I think.

Dave Well, why don't you get a torch or something. I don't want to be carved up by some monster without seeing it.

Corinne Is that meant to be funny, Dave?

Dave (*laughing*)Only if you're the monster!

Vicky There's one in the kitchen.

Dave A monster?

Vicky A *torch*, stupid.

LIGHTS UP

Dave laughs again and the lights suddenly flicker back on. Matt, Emma and Dave are still in their original positions. Apart from Dave and Guy, all their faces still register concern

Corinne (*glancing up at the lights*)Thank heaven for that!

Emma (*after a brief pause, glancing round*)Shall we approach this scientifically? Assuming there *is* a demon in our midst—

Corinne (*irritably*)Oh, come on, Emma!

Emma (*oblivious*)He obviously knows we're talking about him.

Matt (*moving* DL; *pointedly*)Or her.

Emma (*staring at him*)Or her. But though we can't actually see the thing itself, we should be able to pinpoint the person harbouring it.

Guy How?

Emma Well, don't the devil's servants have an aversion to anything holy? And carry an identifying mark of some kind?

Guy (*with mock awe*)Six-Six-Six. The Number of the Beast!

Emma (*to Matt*)They *do*, don't they?

Matt Supposedly.

Emma (*briskly*)Then why don't we have a hand inspection to see if we can find it?

Vicky (*moving to the table behind the sofa*)And pass this round while we do.

She takes a small crucifix from the box which is lying there and holds it up for them to see

Dave (*dryly*)My, my! Every eventuality catered for.

Vicky (*glancing at Emma*)Great minds think alike.

Emma gives a wry smile as Guy moves forward, hands in his pockets

Guy (*nonchalantly*)Yes, but isn't it all a bit impractical?

They stare at him

I mean, any mark could be removed with plastic surgery. Assuming it *is* on the hand and not somewhere else. (*He gestures to the crucifix*)And aversions can be overcome.

Vicky (*firmly*)Even so — let's try it.

Corinne (*suddenly*)No — wait!

They all turn to face her

If there really is a demon here it's extremely dangerous. It would never let you corner it.

Dave (*as the others hesitate*)And from all I've heard, only a formal exorcism can destroy one. (*He gazes round*)Anyone know any friendly exorcists?

Matt Yes. Dr Ciprian, downstairs.

Dave Then I think you ought to fetch her.

Matt (*glancing at his watch and frowning*)She was to be here anyway. Something must have kept her.

Dave Well, let's wait till she turns up, shall we?

There is a noticeable increase in tension

Guy Look — hasn't all this gone a bit far? We're really scaring each other. (*To Matt; attempting to be cheerful*)Tell us it's a joke and let's get on with the party — eh?

Matt (*staring at him gravely*)It's not a joke as far as I'm concerned.

Guy (*looking askance*)But it has to be. Come on, Matt. (*He notices the way everyone is staring at him*) OK then — if there is something here, why didn't it attack us when the lights were out? If it's so bothered about protecting itself it could have done so then and got clean away. But it didn't. And *why*? (*Emphatically*)Because the bloody thing doesn't exist!

Vicky stares at him, then moves down to Matt

Vicky (*quietly but firmly*)I think you should try to find Lucia.

He nods and starts to move UC

Guy (*angrily*)Oh for God's sake! We've known each other for years. If one of us was possessed don't you think we'd have spotted it? Use your head!

He confronts Matt who takes a step away from him

Dave (*softly*)Me thinks the boy protests too much.
Emma (*faintly*)Yes.

Guy glances from face to face then breaks away from Matt, chuckling

Guy OK, OK! Go and fetch your precious doctor, if that's how you feel.

Keeping a watchful eye on him, Matt starts to move towards the doorway UR *but as he reaches it Guy turns to him abruptly, his face serious*

But you'll have trouble getting out. I've locked the door and chucked the key through the letter-box.

Everyone freezes, staring at him with real fear. Corinne rushes to the wall phone

(*turning to her; blandly*)And Corinne — that phone doesn't work anymore.

She stares at him and then at the receiver with its broken wire

Matt moves across to Vicky who is holding the crucifix defensively. Emma rises and moves close to the door DL *as Corinne replaces the receiver, staring fearfully at Guy*

Corinne (*shakily*)What are you going to do?

He turns to face her, his face expressionless, before extending his hands towards her, palms upward

Guy (*evenly*)Take a good look, Corinne. What can you see? There isn't even a *mole*, let alone three little sixes!

She advances warily, before examining his hands carefully. He turns them over so she can see the backs

Corinne (*glancing up*)No, they're no different to mine.

He suddenly grips her forearm and she flinches

Guy (*emphatically*)I'm no demon. (*He turns to the others*)I don't believe *anyone* is!
Emma (*perplexed*)Then why did you lock the door?
Guy I thought you were all playing a game! (*He turns to Matt*) But if you still want to fetch Dr Ciprian, go on. I won't stop you. (*Wryly*)Nor will anything else.

His hand slides down to give Corinne's a reassuring squeeze. During the following dialogue the others start to return to their seats

Matt (*hesitating; slightly embarrassed*)I can't.
Dave Why not?
Matt (*staring at Guy*)He threw the key through the letter-box, didn't he?
Dave Well, surely you have a spare?

Matt That *was* the spare. We lost the other a month ago.

The others suddenly look tense again

Dave (*gesturing* UC)How about the window? Can you get out that way?
Vicky (*sceptically*)Dave—we're six floors up!
Dave But there must be something connecting you with the other flats.
Matt Just a narrow ledge.
Corinne How narrow?
Matt Five inches. (*He glances at the windows*)But even a cat couldn't cross that in this weather. (*With a frown*)We'll just have to break the door down.
Emma Isn't that a bit extreme?

Matt hesitates

You'd be better off waiting for someone to pass by — then call to them to...(*Wryly*) set us free.
Matt (*turning to Vicky*)What d'you think?
Vicky She's right. We don't want to ruin the door for nothing.

They exchange glances for a moment, then he relaxes

Matt No.. OK then — we'll do that. (*At large; brightly*)Who's for another drink?
Dave (*eagerly*)Well, I won't say no.(*He grins*)But do I ever?

Corinne frowns but says nothing

Make it a large one!
Guy (*going to retrieve his glass*)" Each throat was parched, and

glazed each eye..."(*To Matt; grinning*)And mine's a double gin!

Vicky starts moving towards the door UL

Matt Ladies?
Vicky I'll have mine when I get back. I'm going to see about some food.
Emma D'you need a hand?
Vicky (*turning; gratefully*) I wouldn't mind. (*As Emma joins her*)Thanks.

Emma and Vicky exit UL

Matt hands Dave a fresh glass of whisky, then turns to Corinne who seems lost in thought

Matt Same again, Corinne?
Corinne (*rousing herself*)Yes, please — but make sure Dave doesn't over do it. (*She turns to Dave*)I don't want to carry you home on my shoulder.
Dave (*suggestively*)You'd rather I did that to you — eh?
Corinne (*tolerantly*)Don't be silly.

She saunters out UL, *having picked up her evening bag*

Guy (*staring after her*)You're a lucky man, Dave.
Dave Yeah?
Guy Corinne's a real stunner. Where was it you found her? Abroad?
Dave (*rising and moving to the door* DL)On that last European trip (*He grimaces*)The only good thing about it. The days were hell. (*He grins*)But the nights were bloody spectacular!

Guy I'll bet.

Dave exits

Guy watches Dave exit, then turns to Matt as he hands him his drink

How long d' you reckon it'll last?
Matt What?
Guy (*gesturing* DL)Dave and Corinne. You know him—he changes girls faster than we change shirts!
Matt (*slowly*)He told me he wants to settle down.
Guy (*laughing*)The hell he does! He only stays long enough to—
Matt (*suddenly*)Guy — what made you rip the phone out?

Guy stares at him silently

Wasn't that a bit much — (*Pointedly*) for a joke?
Guy (*after another pause*)You're right. (*He grins feebly*)But it was pitch-black in here and I guess I don't know my own strength. (*Apologetically*)Sorry, mate.

Matt grunts noncommittally and then knocks back his drink

As he does, Lucia Ciprian appears in the doorway UR. *Dressed as Corinne described her, she presents a slightly eccentric image, but her manner is mature and intelligent. She appears to be in her late thirties and when she speaks it is with a mid-European accent. She carries an intricately worked shoulder bag*

Matt (*catching sight of her as he lowers his glass*)Lucia! How did you —?

Lucia (*quickly*)I found the key outside and thought there might be trouble. (*She glances at Guy*)Is there?

Matt (*also glancing at Guy*)Not exactly.

Lucia (*dryly*)You don't sound too sure. (*She takes a couple of steps towards* C, *then halts, her face serious*)It's here again.

Matt looks immediately wary, but Guy steps forward quizzically

Guy What is?

Lucia (*turning to Matt*)The presence I warned you about. It's definitely here.

Guy (*glancing from one the other*)You're joking!

Lucia (*oblivious*)Except... it's much stronger than I expected it to be. (*She runs a hand through her hair in a bewildered fashion*)

Matt (*sharply*)What d'you mean?

Lucia (*extending her arms as if to feel the air*)Much stronger. (*Perplexed*)I don't understand. (*Abruptly she turns to face Matt*)Where are the others?

Matt(*gesturing up* L)They've gone to sort out some food. (*With a note of desperation*)Look here — I don't mean to put you down, Lucia, but ... the things you've talked about — are you absolutely sure they're true?

Lucia (*pointedly*)If I hadn't been, I wouldn't be here — and if we don't take proper precautions everyone in this flat is in great danger. The elemental has certainly caused one death tonight, and while the full moon drives it, it may do so again.

Guy (*with a touch of exasperation*)But you're talking about *devils*, Doctor. The kind of thing you only see in books!

Lucia (*emphatically*)And how do they come to *be* there? If devils don't exist who had the vision to depict them — as people have consistently done the whole world over? You can't tell me that such a universal image is a figment of the imagination!

Guy (*hesitating*)It might be. We all have the same kind of dreams or nightmares. Don't we?

Lucia Yes — but rarely does a dream result in dead bodies being strewn in alleys and subways!

There is a momentary pause, then Guy laughs sceptically

Guy So you seriously believe that someone here isn't just possessed, which is daft enough in itself — they're a mass murderer, too?

Lucia I do. (*She stares him out*)And when I find that person — I'm going to destroy him.

Guy Well, don't waste time on me. (*He places his fingers on either side of his head*)My horns are well hidden.

Matt (*trying to stall him*)Guy...

Guy (*mischievously*)Or maybe you're looking for something else? (*He turns away from them, bending down slightly*)Hey, Matt! Is this a tail— Or a ruck in my boxer shorts?

Lucia (*dryly*)Evil doesn't sport such obvious attributes, you know. The force we're dealing with is quite normal in appearance — except for those brief moments when it's alone with its victim.

Matt And then?

Lucia The demon takes over the mind and body of its host, forcing him to do unspeakable things.

Guy (*incredulously*)Oh God — I can't credit this!

He moves towards the door UL, *laughing harshly*

Lucia (*evenly*)You really should. For your own sake.

Guy (*pause; dryly*)" And some in dreams assurèd were of the Spirit that plagued us so..." (*He jabs his chest*)Me — I'm a realist!

He exits

Lucia turns to Matt, who is frowning heavily

Lucia What's worrying you?

Matt (*hesitantly*)Those girls — the ones who've been murdered — they were strangers. No one here had anything to do with them.

Lucia You're wrong. One person, at least, knew all four.

Matt (*askance*)How ?

Lucia (*seating herself on the sofa*)Maria Estevez, the first victim, was a high-class call-girl known to a great many businessmen in this area. (*She pauses*) Businessmen like yourself.

Matt (*awkwardly*)Maybe, but that doesn't mean —

Lucia (*interrupting him*)Lucy Danforth used to be a waitress in the Ten High Club.

Matt suddenly looks uncomfortable

You know it?

Matt (*nodding*)I've been there a couple of times.

Lucia (*relentlessly*)And Evelyn Walker, a very pretty masseuse — until a month ago — worked in an establishment quite close to your firm. (*Pointedly*)Again, you must have known about it?

Matt Well, yes, but... (*Sharply*)Look, *I* never went there.

Lucia (*smiling wryly*) I'm sure you didn't. But someone else here did.

Matt Who?

Lucia (*oblivious*)Tonight's victim — it's just been revealed — was a young woman named Caroline Forbes.

The news comes as a shock to Matt

Matt *Caroline* ?
Lucia You know her?
Matt (*with difficulty*)Yes! She's ...she was... Dave's *secretary* !
Lucia (*sharply*)Dave? Is he one of the people here tonight?

Matt nods and then freezes, staring at her with sudden fear

Matt You spoke to him down in the foyer, remember?

Lucia's eyes widen

You told him he was in danger. (*His voice rises*)But you got
it wrong! *He's* the one who —   BLACK OUT ✳

Abruptly the lights fail and the room is plunged into darkness

Matt (*angrily*)Oh bloody hell!

*Before he can say anything there is a high-pitched terrified
scream from off L*

Lucia (*urgently*)Who's that?
Matt (*realizing*)It's Vicky! (*He shouts*)Vicky !

*He heads for the door DL in the darkness and thuds against it
heavily*

What the — ? The bloody door's locked!
Lucia (*faintly*)Good God!
Matt (*pounding on the door*)Will someone get this thing open!
Emma (*off UL*)Matt! Where are you?

LIGHTS UP

Matt (*still hammering*)Stop fooling about in there!

Just as suddenly the lights blaze again, causing Lucia and Matt to blink briefly and then another scream is heard from Corinne

Emma (*rushing in from* UL)What's going on?
Matt (*banging on the door*)Open the door! For God's sake, open it!

    The door swings open to reveal Guy supporting an ashen-faced Corinne. Their hands are clearly blood-stained

Corinne (*reaching out blindly*)Matt...
Emma (*clapping a hand to her mouth; horrified*)Oh God!
Matt (*with difficulty*)Where's Vicky?

    Matt rushes out L

Guy In the bathroom. But wait!

Corinne moans and then slumps in Guy's arms

Guy Christ — she's fainted. Give me a hand, will you, Em?

Together they move her to the armchair L

Lucia (*sharply*)She's not hurt?
Guy (*glancing up*)No, but—
Emma (*to Corinne as she stirs*)Just sit still. Don't try to move.
Lucia What happened in there?
Guy (*bleakly*)You don't want to know.

She stares at him sharply, then turns as

Matt enters, escorting Vicky, who is sobbing wretchedly. Her hands and face are also smeared with blood

Emma (*straightening up, her voice shaky*)I think things have gone far enough — don't you, Matt?
Matt (*grimly*)Damn right, they have. (*He gestures off* L) Dave's in the bathroom — with a skewer through his throat!

Lucia and Emma both look horrified

Lucia (*faintly*)Dear God!
Vicky (*hysterically*)I saw it! I saw it do it to him! It was horrible!

She shudders convulsively, clutching his arm

Matt (*gently stroking her hair*)I wouldn't talk about it.
Vicky (*wide-eyed*)But I have to. They've got to know! (*She pulls herself together and moves* C *gazing at each of them in turn*) I went to the bathroom to wash my hands — after we'd finished the food — and I forgot to lock the door. I'd only been there a minute when Dave came in and started — pawing me.

She looks at Matt for reassurance and he nods gently. Guy and Corinne exchange glances and then she lowers her head sadly

Vicky (*swallowing*)And then the lights went out. I tried to get away from him, but he followed — and this time he really put his hands on me. (*She breaks off, wide-eyed*)And that's when it happened...
Lucia (*urgently*)What did?
Vicky Something — or someone — sprang through the bathroom door and dragged him away from me!

Her voice breaks and she puts her hands over her face. Matt crosses to put his arm around her, obviously concerned

Emma (*pointedly*)A man or a woman?

Vicky I don't know. All I saw were the eyes — yellow and glittering, as if — as if they were lit from inside!

Corinne (*faintly*)The demon.

Vicky (*nodding*)It must have been. But then it was gone, dragging Dave into the bedroom. I could hear him struggling, but it must have had its hand over his face because he didn't cry out. And then it— it — I heard the sound of the skewer going through his throat and — oh, God! — it pushed his body back at me, knocking me over!

She moans and buries her face in Matt's chest. The others stare at each other silently for a moment

Emma (*faintly*)So it really does exist.

Guy (*grimly*)Yes and the bugger nearly flattened me trying to get out!

Lucia (*sharply*)Of where?

Guy (*gesturing* L)The bedroom.

Matt (*suspiciously*)You were in there, too?

Guy (*easily*) I was on my way to take a leak— but the thing hit me just as I stepped through the door.

Lucia Do you know where it went?

Guy Out into the passage, I guess. But which *way* ...

He shrugs helplessly

Lucia (*turning to Corinne*)Where were you when all this was happening?

Corinne (*quietly*)In the spare bedroom. (*She glances at Emma and Vicky*)I'd gone to touch up my lipstick — and when Vicky screamed I ran down and collided with Guy. (*She turns to Guy*) Didn't I?

Guy nods

Matt No-one passed you on the way?

Corinne No. (*Suddenly*)But it might have gone the other way — towards the kitchen

Emma (*emphatically*)It didn't. I stayed there after you and Vicky left, and no-one came near it.

Matt (*realizing*)And when Vicky screamed you came straight in here.

Emma (*nodding*)Yes.

Lucia (*pointedly*)Well... whoever it was — and whichever way they went — I know where they are now.

Corinne (*wide-eyed*)In here. (*She stares round*)One of us. (*She turns to Lucia; desperately*)But why should they want to kill Dave? I don't understand. Why *him*?

Lucia (*evenly*)Why anyone?

Corinne stares at her and then begins to cry helplessly

Matt (*heading* UR*; determinedly*)I'm going for help.

Lucia I'm afraid you can't, Matt.

Matt (*turning*)Why not?

Lucia I've locked us all in.

Emma (*incredulously*)Oh, not again!

Guy (*dryly*)This is getting a mite tedious, wouldn't you say?

Matt (unperturbed)Then we'll just have to force our way out. Come on, Guy!

*During the following exchange Corinne rises and makes her
way unobtrusively to the door* UL *through which she exits*

Vicky (*hurrying to Matt and restraining him*)No! It will kill you
if you touch that door, I know it! (*As Matt hesitates*)Don't,
Matt. Please!

Matt stares at her and then Lucia

Lucia I advise you to listen to her. (*Firmly*)Besides — I think we
can resolve this without outside help.
Guy (*puzzled*)How?
Emma (*glancing round; sharply*)Where's Corinne?

She hurries to open the door DL, *peering off as Guy does the same*
UL. *He reacts immediately to what he sees*

Guy (*calling off*) Corinne! What the hell d'you think you're
doing?!
Corinne (*off; faintly*)What you lot are too *scared* to do. I'm
going for the police!
Guy (*to the others as they rush forward*)Jesus Christ! She's gone
out through the window!
Vicky (*calling desperately*)But that ledge is dangerous! You'll
fall!
Corinne (*off; faintly*)Oh no, I won't !
Matt She's trying to get to the window of the stairwell.
Emma How far's that?
Matt About twenty feet. (*Urgently*)Vicky—keep an eye on her
through the other windows!

Vicky nods and hurries out UL *followed by Emma*

Lucia (*to Matt*)Will she be able to make it?
Matt I think so. If she's very careful.

He turns to glance at them both, running his fingers through his hair distractedly

Only five of us now — and one's a killer.
Guy (*smiling grimly*)Waiting for the next power-cut.

As he and Matt stare at each other, Lucia moves quietly to the door UL *and locks it*

Lucia (*turning with the key in her hand*)Now there are only three
of us.

The men stare at her in amazement

And if I go into the bedroom and lock both doors, there'll only
be two. Which means the demon can only claim one more
victim — and if it does, it'll be forced to reveal itself.
Guy (*irritably*)And what good will that do?
Matt (*rounding on him*)Can you think of anything better?

Guy hesitates

Anyway, it's only till Corinne gets here with —

A shrill scream of utter terror rings out from behind the door UL
*and they all freeze. But not for long. Matt and Guy both rush
towards the door, but Lucia gets there first, barring their way*

Matt (*furious*)Let me past, damn you! Vicky's in there!

He tries to pull Lucia away from the door

Guy (*urgently*)And Emma!

Matt (*to Lucia*)If you don't unlock that door, I'll kill you!

Lucia (*raising a hand imperatively*)Wait! If I do the demon will come out. Do *you*
want to die too?

They pause momentarily

What's happened in there is finished. We can't do anything about it. But we've got to stop the same thing happening to us. Surely you see that?

Matt's hands fall to his side in despair

Guy (*gesturing to the door; urgently*)But which one of them is it?

Matt (*dully*)Not Vicky... because she saw it kill Dave. (*He raises his eyes*)It's Emma. *She's* the demon.

Guy (*incredulous*)No ... she can't be.

Matt I'm telling you, Guy —

There is a sudden pounding on the door behind them and they all recoil

Guy (*involuntarily*)Oh Jesus! (*The pounding is repeated*)What are we going to do?

Lucia opens her shoulder bag and produces a small revolver

Lucia (*deliberately*)I think, perhaps we'd *better* open the door.

Matt (*pointing to the gun*)But what use will that be against —

whatever's in there?
Guy Yes. I didn't think bullets counted.
Lucia Normal bullets, no.
Guy (*puzzled*)Then what — ?
Lucia They're silver. *Holy* silver. (*She hands the key to Matt*)
Open the door, please — then step away from it. Quickly.

*After a momentary hesitation he moves to the door and unlocks
it. Then, cautiously, he puts hand on the knob and jerks the door
violently open, jumping back out of the line of fire*

*It is Corinne who steps across the threshold, with dishevelled
hair and clenched hands. Everyone stares at her in amazement*

Corinne (*quietly*)Don't worry. Everything's all right.

Matt and Guy rush out of the room

Lucia keeps her gun trained on Corinne, staring at her fixedly

Lucia (*evenly*)I'm glad to hear it.

Matt enters quickly, clearly relieved

Matt They've passed out, that's all.

Lucia nods as Matt grabs a brandy bottle and hurries out again

Lucia (*to Corinne*)What happened to you?

As Corinne is speaking Guy enters quietly behind her

Corinne (*hesitantly*)I couldn't make it to the staircase. (*She* *gestures feebly to the windows*)All that wind and rain. I was scared. So I came back in.(*Suddenly*)What happened in there?

Lucia Don't you know?

Corinne (*puzzled*)No. I just saw Vicky and Emma lying on the kitchen floor.

As Guy is speaking Matt and Vicky enter UL *and stand listening, clearly astonished at what they hear*

Guy (*harshly*)You're a liar, Corinne.

Corinne (*turning; startled*)What?

Guy They're there because you tried to attack them!

Corinne No!

Guy Who else could it have been? (*He gestures*)The rest of us were in here!

Corinne (*strangely bewildered*)Guy...

Guy (*relentlessly*)*You* were the one who killed all those girls. *Because Dave was having it off with them* ! We all know what he was like. (*Sharply*)But you couldn't stand it — the thought of him with other women — so you got rid of them one by one!

Matt (*askance*)But why in heaven's name would she kill Dave?

Guy (*grimly*)Because she heard him in the bathroom — with Vicky. (*Rounding on her*)That was the last straw, wasn't it? And the demon that's been driving you made you grab a skewer and stick it through his neck!

Corinne (*desperately*)No! (*To Lucia*)Don't listen to him!

Guy (*at large; gesturing to Lucia*)For God's sake — that's why she tried to warn him! (*He turns to Lucia*)Isn't it?

Lucia (*staring at him strangely*)Yes, but ... how do you know all this?

At this point Emma suddenly enters UL, *pushing past Matt and Vicky*

Emma (*apprehensively*)Dr Ciprian!

*As Lucia turns to look at her Corinne throws herself forward with
an enraged scream and knocks the woman off her feet. The gun
flies across the room and Matt scrambles to pick it up as Lucia
does her best to fend off Corinne's slashing nails*

Emma (*appalled*) Dear God! *Stop her* !
Matt (*advancing, gun in hand*)Let her go,Corinne! I'm
   warning you! I'll —

*Before he can finish Corinne raises a face savage with fury and
launches herself at him, but then he fires two shots which cause
her to fall limply to the floor. Lucia picks herself up unsteadily,
stepping away from Corinne as she tries to raise her head*

Corinne (*lifting a hand and pointing to Guy*)You bastard! You
   ... traitor...(*With difficulty*)I thought you loved me...
Vicky (*warily*)What's she saying?
Guy (*curtly*)She's raving, that's all.
Lucia (*peremptorily*)Ssh!
Corinne (*coughing*)Get him! Before it's too late. (*Urgently*)Go
   on — *shoot him* !

*Confused, but with his gun hand steady, Matt looks from Corinne
to Guy, whose face is expressionless*

Lucia Why?
Corinne (*emphatically*)He's in league with me! (*There is a
   dreadful pause*)Didn't you *sense* it?
Lucia (*faintly; realizing*)So that's why the aura was so strong.
Corinne (*nodding*)Because there were *two* demons — not one!
   (*With increasing difficulty*)I killed those girls, yes. (*She points
   to Guy again*)But *he* was the one who killed Dave — because

he wanted me for himself! (*Bitterly*)Or so I thought...
Guy (*with an odd smile*)Needs must when the devil drives.
Corinne (*as the others react to this*)Take a look at his hands! The
   mark's on *both* of them. Six-Six-Six!

Guy starts to back away, his face tense

   For God's sake — *don't let him get away* !   — START TAPE

*This last effort is too much for her and she falls back on the floor.
Guy gives a strange laugh and raises his arms above his head as
Lucia and Matt start to move towards him*

Guy (*his voice evil*)Too late, my love. *Much* too late!

*A terrific thunder-clap is heard and the room is plunged into
darkness. Someone screams in terror as the sound of breaking
glass is heard, followed by a howling gale, and then Guy's voice
is heard again — fiendishly triumphant*

Guy My dear Corinne, so beautiful. And she now dead did lie.
   " But a thousand, thousand slimy things lived on — and so did
   I! "

CURTAIN

FURNITURE AND PROPERTY LIST

On stage : Shelf units. *On them* : hi-fi equipment, *objets d'art* and a collection of drinks and glasses
Bookcase. *In it* : assortment of books *On it* : attractive modern clock
Wall phone
Table. *On it* : photographs and a carved wooden box containing a crucifix
Two-seater sofa
Two armchairs
Two side tables
Key in door up L
Framed prints
Rug

Off stage : Carrier bag containing mixers for drinks (**Vicky**)
Ice bucket (**Guy**)
Water
Stage blood

Personal : **Corinne**: evening bag
Matt: wrist-watch
Guy: wrist-watch
Dr Ciprian: shoulder bag. *In it*: a small revolver

LIGHTING PLOT

Property fittings required: pendant light
Interior. The same throughout

To open : General lighting

Cue 1	**Matt** turns away to refill his glass *Lights flicker and then go out*	(Page 14)
Cue 2	**Dave** laughs again *Lights flicker and revert to previous lighting*	(Page 14)
Cue 3	**Matt:** "*He's* the one who — " *Abruptly the lights fail and the room is plunged into darkness*	(Page 25)
Cue 4	**Matt:** " Stop fooling about in there!" *Suddenly the lights blaze again*	(Page 26)
Cue 5	A terrific thunder clap is heard *The room is plunged into darkness*	(Page 36)

EFFECTS PLOT

Cue 1   To open   (Page 1)
Heavy rain is heard lashing against windows

Cue 2   **Guy**: "... roared and howled." Vicky listens (Page 3)
The door buzzer sounds

Cue 3   **Vicky** disappears through the doorway   (Page 3)
Sound of door being opened

Cue 4   **Emma**: " If Dave tries any of his lechy little tricks
tonight —"   (Page 5)
The door buzzer sounds again

Cue 5   **Vicky** disappears. **Emma** sips her drink   (Page 6)
Sound of door being opened

Cue 6   **Guy** : " What?"   (Page 8)
Door buzzer sounds

Cue 7   **Guy**: " Too late, my love. *Much* too late!" (Page36)
A terrific thunder-clap

Cue 8   Someone screams in terror   (Page 36)
*Sound of breaking glass is heard followed by a
    howling gale*